M000017189

TO

WITH

Love

ALSO BY ALLEN APPEL

To My Husband with Love

Old Dog's Guide for Pups

Thanks, Dad

Thanks, Mom

TO

My Wife

WITH

Love

Allen Appel

ST. MARTIN'S PRESS NEW YORK

www.stmartins.com

Book design by Judith Stagnitto Abbate

ISBN 0-312-28496-9

First Edition: February 2002

10   9   8   7   6   5   4   3   2   1

TO

My Wife

WITH

Love

———— ... ————

Thanks, Dear,

FOR . . .

Thanks, Dear, for...

——————— ... ———————

*G*oing out with me that first time.

Thanks, Dear, for...

...

Going out with me the second time.

Thanks, Dear, for...

--- ... ---

Choosing me when there were plenty
of other guys to choose from.

Finding me interesting.

Finding me attractive.

Thanks, Dear, for...

...

Not making fun of my proposal.

Thanks, Dear, for...

---... ---

Accepting my proposal.

Thanks, Dear, for...

——— ... ———

*A*greeing to marry me even after
you met my mother.

Thanks, Dear, for...

*B*eing a beautiful bride.

*N*ot being jealous of my former girlfriends and/or wives. Believe me, none of them did, could, or ever would hold a candle to you.

*B*eing endlessly fascinating.

*T*alking.

*L*istening.

Thanks, Dear, for...

Being glad to see me.

Thanks, Dear, for...

...

Being good company.

Thanks, Dear, for...

——— ... ———

Participating.

Thanks, Dear, for...

--- ... ---

*P*articipating enthusiastically in
activities I like to do that you might
not be naturally inclined toward.

Thanks, Dear, for...

...

*C*aring and consoling. Even tough
guys like me need it every once
in a while.

Thanks, Dear, for...

--- ... ---

$\mathcal{B}$eing nice, even when I'm in a
bad mood.

Being nice when I need
a kind word.

Being patient.

Being kind.

*G*iving me the benefit of your
wisdom.

Sometimes I don't act like I appreciate
it, but I do.

$\mathcal{T}hanks, \; Dear, \; for \ldots$

...

$\mathcal{C}$leaning the house. I know I could
do more in that area and I'm going to
try really really hard to help out.

No, really. Honest.
What are you laughing about?

*C*ooking for me.

*C*ooking for my family when they
come over. And don't pay any
attention to what my mother says, she
doesn't mean it.

Thanks, Dear, for...

—————— ... ——————

*C*ooking things that I like but you're
not crazy about.

*C*ooking year in, year out, and never
(hardly) complaining about it.

Cooking some of the things my
mom used to cook.

Putting up with my cooking.

*H*aving faith in my ability to
fix household items, even though it
usually isn't warranted. It's this
kind of blind faith that keeps
men going.

*D*oing most of the shopping.
Okay, all of the shopping.

GROCERIES

*P*utting up with my snoring.

Thanks, Dear, for...

...

*P*utting up with my weird relatives.

Thanks, Dear, for...

———————— ... ————————

*P*utting up with some of my friends
that I know you don't care for. They're
not going to lead me astray. Honest.

... ...

Not seeming to mind my lack
of hair.

Thanks, Dear, for...

—————— ... ——————

*S*aying you're sorry.

*N*ot rubbing it in when you're right
and I'm wrong.

Thanks, Dear, for...

...

*A*ccepting my apologies.

Thanks, Dear, for...

...

Forgiving me.

Thanks, Dear, for...

...

*F*orgiving me again. And again.

*H*earing me out.

Thanks, Dear, for...

— ... —

*K*nowing what I mean, even when
it's not what I say.

Thanks, Dear, for...

...

$\mathcal{B}$eing nice even when I'm a jackass.

Thanks, Dear, for...

———————— ... ————————

*D*iscussing things reasonably, even
when I'm not being reasonable.

Sticking with me, even when you think I'm doing something foolish.

Thanks, Dear, for...

———————— ... ————————

*N*ot stopping me when I'm about
to do something you think is foolish.

Stopping me when I'm about to do something *incredibly* foolish.

Thanks, Dear, for...

---------- ... ----------

*N*ot telling my secrets.

*S*uffering in silence.
Most of the time.

Not rolling your eyes at me.
Too much. I know I do goofy stuff
sometimes.

Thanks, Dear, for...

——————— ... ———————

*D*eferring to me when I'm right.

*D*eferring to me when I'm wrong
but need the ego reinforcement.
(It's a Man Thing.)

*N*ot doing what you sometimes
must feel like doing.

Thanks, Dear, for...

— ... —

$\mathcal{N}$ot harboring grudges
(at least not for long).

Thanks, Dear, for...

——————— ... ———————

Keeping me on course. Gently.
Sometimes even a man as wise as I
needs a good navigator.

Thanks, Dear, for...

...

$\mathcal{N}$ot making fun of my
brainstorms.

$\mathcal{N}$ot dragging up past brainstorm
failures.

Thanks, Dear, for...

———— ... ————

*P*articipating in some of my wackier
brainstorms.

Thanks, Dear, for...

---...---

Giving me advice about my work.
I don't always take it, but I always
consider it carefully.

Thanks, Dear, for...

--- ... ---

*T*aking care of me when I'm sick.

*T*aking care of me when I'm not really sick but just feel like having someone take care of me. It never lasts for long.

*R*epairing me when I'm injured.

*N*ot saying, "You're too
(old, fat, out-of-shape) to be . . ."
doing whatever I was doing when I
injured myself.

Thanks, Dear, for...

--- ... ---

*N*ot criticizing my driving.

*N*ot making me stop and ask for directions.

*N*ot making fun of me when I get us lost.

Thanks, Dear, for...

--- ... ---

*N*ot treating me the way some of
your friends treat their husbands.

Thanks, Dear, for...

...

*T*reating me like royalty.

Thanks, Dear, for...

· ... ·

*B*eing proud of
my accomplishments,
even though they may be small.

Thanks, Dear, for...

·...·

Your sense of humor.

Making me laugh.

Thanks, Dear, for...

...

Sharing a good laugh.

Thanks, Dear, for...

---

*R*emembering my birthday.

*G*iving me presents.

Thanks, Dear, for...

...

Giving me presents that
I actually like.

Not being too hard on me when I
forget:
Birthdays
Anniversaries
Sizes

Thanks, Dear, for...

*L*etting me do things I like to do
without giving me grief. Usually.

Thanks, Dear, for...

...
---

*N*ot complaining (too much) when
I buy important electronic devices even
though you think we don't need them.

Thanks, Dear, for...

———— ... ————

*N*agging, when it's important.

*N*ot nagging when it isn't.

*G*iving me time to myself.

Thanks, Dear, for...

...

*L*etting me have nights out
with the guys.

$\mathcal{B}$eing fairly reasonable when
things get a little out of hand.

Thanks, Dear, for...

———— ... ————

*B*eing the designated driver.

*B*eing the designated driver even though we agreed that it was my turn.

Thanks, Dear, for...

························

*L*istening to my stories, even
though you've heard them all before.
And still laughing in all the right
places.

Thanks, Dear, for...

——— ... ———

*U*nderstanding.

*P*retending to understand, even if
you don't.

*H*elping me pick out my ties.

*H*elping me pick out clothing in general. You know how much I hate shopping for my own stuff.

Thanks, Dear, for...

--- ... ---

Taking great care of me even though
I don't deserve it.

Thanks, Dear, for...

— ... —

Making me go to the dentist, get
my hair cut, go to the doctor, and all
the other things I don't like, but
ought, to do.

*C*arrying more than your share of
the load.

Thanks, Dear, for...

———— ... ————

$\mathcal{S}$ex. Everything about sex.

$\mathcal{T}$hat first time.

$\mathcal{S}$howing me what you like
(and don't like).

Thanks, Dear, for...

<hr>

... ...

<hr>

*B*eing romantic.

Thanks, Dear, for...

...

Surprising me.

$\mathcal{B}$eing so delectable.

Thanks, Dear, for...

...

Being such a babe.

Thanks, Dear, for...

---··· ···

Being enthusiastic.

Thanks, Dear, for...

... .

Seducing me.

Thanks, Dear, for...

———————— ... ————————

*C*heerfully indulging my fantasies.

Thanks, Dear, for...

—— ··· ——

Actively participating in my fantasies.

Thanks, Dear, for...

...

$\mathcal{N}$ot minding if I look at the ladies,
because you know I'd never touch.

PRETTY
LADIES

$\mathcal{K}$eeping fit. For both of us.
Or at least thinking about it. We'll
start soon.

...

*A*lways smelling so nice.

*A*lways looking nice.
To me you are always beautiful.

Thanks, Dear, for...

·:·

Still admiring me after all
these years.

Thanks, Dear, for...

...

*B*eing proud of me.

*B*eing my friend.

Thanks, Dear, for...

--- ... ---

Making me happy. Keeping me happy. Being happy.

Thanks, Dear, for...

...

*Y*our faithfulness to me.

*Y*our faith in me.

*Y*our faith in the two of us.

Thanks, Dear, for...

—————— ... ——————

*L*oving me.

*F*orever.